Meet the Family

My Mom

by Mary Auld

Gareth Stevens Publishing
A WORLD ALMANAC EDUCATION GROUP COMPANY

This is Darren
and his mother.
Sometimes he calls
her Mommy, but
mostly he just calls
her Mom.

Sally grew inside
her mother for nine
months before she
was born.

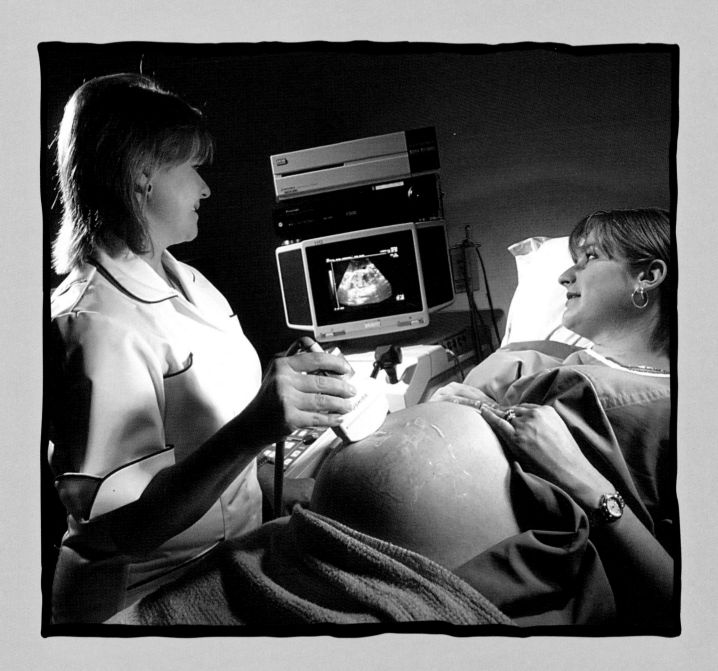

Jake was adopted when he was ten weeks old. His mom has loved him ever since.

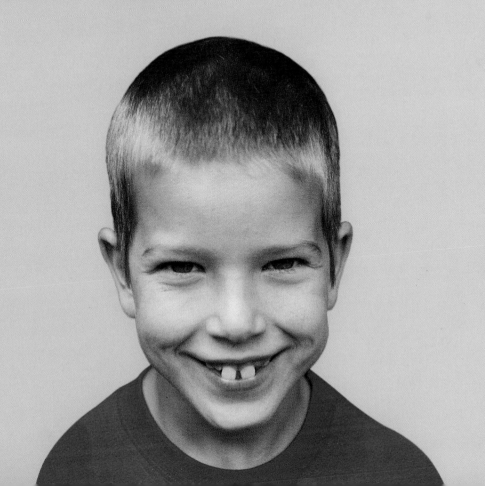

Lizzie has two moms. Her stepmom is married to her dad now. Lizzie lives with her stepmom and dad on weekends.

David's mom works in a hospital.

Chai's mom works
in an office.

Susan's mom
is a teacher.

Jason's mom works at
home, caring for him
and his baby brother.

Polly's parents take turns picking her up from school. Her mom picks her up Mondays, Wednesdays, and Fridays.

Mary Jo likes going
shopping with her mom.

Ahmed likes it when he and his mom play in the park.

Paula's mom makes dinner when she gets home from work.

Ben and Emma's mom
tucks them in at night.
She tells good stories.

19

This is Maria with her mom and grandma. Grandma is Maria's mom's mom.

What is your mom like?

Family Words

Here are some words people use when talking about their mom or family.

Names for mom:
mother, mommy, mom, mama, parent.

Names for dad:
father, daddy, dad, papa, parent.

Names of other relatives:
son, daughter, brother, sister,
grandchild, grandparent, grandmother,
grandma, grandfather, grandpa,
uncle, aunt, nephew, niece.

A step relative is a person who is related
by a parent's remarriage, not by birth.

When people are adopted, they become part of a family
even though they were not born into that family.

A Family Tree

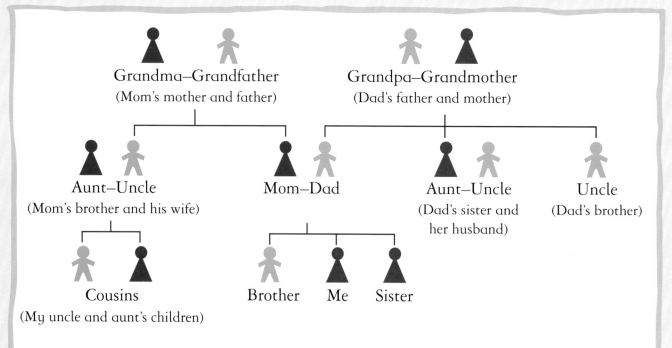

Grandma–Grandfather
(Mom's mother and father)

Grandpa–Grandmother
(Dad's father and mother)

Aunt–Uncle
(Mom's brother and his wife)

Mom–Dad

Aunt–Uncle
(Dad's sister and
her husband)

Uncle
(Dad's brother)

Cousins
(My uncle and aunt's children)

Brother   Me   Sister

You can show how you are related to all your family
on a plan like this one. It is called a family tree.
Every family tree is different. Try drawing your own.

Please visit our web site at: www.garethstevens.com
For a free color catalog describing Gareth Stevens Publishing's list of high-quality
books and multimedia programs, call 1-800-542-2595 (USA) or 1-800-387-3178
(Canada). Gareth Stevens Publishing's fax: (414) 332-3567.

Library of Congress Cataloging-in-Publication Data available upon request from publisher.
Fax (414) 336-0157 for the attention of the Publishing Records Department.

ISBN 0-8368-3927-7

This North American edition first published in 2004 by **Gareth Stevens Publishing**,
A World Almanac Education Group Company, 330 West Olive Street, Suite 100,
Milwaukee, WI 53212 USA

This U.S. edition copyright © 2004 by Gareth Stevens, Inc. First published in 2003 by
Franklin Watts, 96 Leonard Street, London EC2A 4XD. Original copyright © 2003 by
Franklin Watts.

Series editor: Rachel Cooke
Art director: Jonathan Hair
Design: Andrew Crowson
Gareth Stevens editor: Betsy Rasmussen
Gareth Stevens art direction: Tammy Gruenewald

Picture Credits: Peter Beck/Corbis: 11. Bruce Berman/Corbis: front cover center below.
www.johnbirdsall.co.uk: front cover center top, 6, 7, 10, 12, 18. Deep Light Productions/
Science Photo Library: 5. Dex Images Inc/Corbis: 20-21. George Disario/Corbis: 2.
Carlos Goldin/Corbis: front cover center above. Don Mason/Corbis: 1, 13. Brian Mitchell/
Photofusion: 15, 19. Jose Luis Pelaez/Corbis: front cover bottom. Ulrike Press/Format: 17.
George Shelley/Corbis: front cover main, 22. Ariel Skelley/Corbis: front cover center, 8.
Christa Stadtler/Photofusion: 16. While every attempt has been made to clear copyright,
should there be any inadvertent omission please notify the publisher regarding rectification.

Printed in Hong Kong/China

1 2 3 4 5 6 7 8 9 08 07 06 05 04